CW00410675

The Official Book

Jeremy Mark

Virgin

First published in 1999 by
Virgin Books
An imprint of
Virgin Publishing Ltd
Thames Wharf Studios
Rainville Road
London
W6 9HT

Copyright © 1999 B★Witched
Text by Jeremy Mark
Copyright in design and layout © 1999 Virgin Publishing

This book is sold subject to the condition that it shall not,
by way of trade or otherwise, be lent, resold, hired out or
otherwise circulated without the publisher's prior written
consent in any form or binding other than that in which it
is published and without a similar condition being
imposed upon the subsequent purchaser.

A catalogue record for the book is available from the
British Library.

ISBN 0 7535 0351 4

Printed and bound by Butler & Tanner Ltd,
Frome and London

Designed by DW Design

Contents

Introduction
7

CHAPTER ONE: Let The Fun Begin!
8
B★Witched — the early days

CHAPTER TWO: Edele
14

CHAPTER THREE: We'll Give You Such A Thrill!
20
B★Witched's rollercoaster of success begins

CHAPTER FOUR: Lindsay
26
B★Witched Around The World!
32

CHAPTER FIVE: To You We Belong!
34
B★Witched on their fans, lingerie and,
erm, butter!

CHAPTER SIX: Keavy
42

CHAPTER SEVEN: Rollercoaster Of Love
48
B★Witched talk dating, kissing and flirting tips!

CHAPTER EIGHT: Sinéad
53

CHAPTER NINE: We Four Girls Are Here To Stay!
58
What does the future hold for B★Witched?

25 B★Witching Facts!
62
Grab your cap and grab your runners for some amazing secrets!

B★Witched Discography
64

Hi Everybody!

Welcome to the very first official B'Witched book!

We've had an absolutely incredible first year – none of us expected to achieve so much, even in our wildest dreams! – and this book tells our complete story so far.

When we were first asked to write a book we didn't have a clue what to put in it, but when we actually sat down and began to write, all the stories came racing back to us! Find out what we were like at school, how B'Witched all started and how nervous we were before our first TV appearance. Oh, and there's also the embarrassing baby photos our mams have specially dug out, which'll give you a really good laugh! As you can imagine, we've had great fun putting this all together!

Most importantly though, we'd like to say a big THANKS to all of you, because without your continuous support B'Witched wouldn't be where we are today. Thanks a million – and the luck of the Irish to you!

Well, we've got to go now – another plane to catch (we've hardly had time to catch our breath since "C'est La Vie!") So, we hope you enjoy our story and look forward to seeing you again very soon.

Lots of love and stars,

Lindsay   *Sinéad*

B★WITCHED

B★WITCHED

CHAPTER ONE

Let the fun begin

 Lindsay

Starting from the beginning, I guess all four of us knew each other to say 'hello' to around the Digges Lane Dance Centre, long before we even decided to get together and form a group. The Dance Centre was the ideal place for anyone who wanted to learn or practise any form of dancing or entertaining.

Well, back in 1996, Keavy was working as a trainee mechanic in her dad's garage when Sinéad dropped in with her mum, who was having her car fixed. The two girls got chatting and realised that they both wanted to do the same thing: perform. Meanwhile, I had become friends with Keavy through kick-boxing classes, and we'd also talked about putting a pop group together. It had always been Edele's dream to be part of a band too, so the four of us arranged to meet up to talk about it. We all clicked instantly as we could see in each other the determination and drive to really go for it and fulfil our dreams.

Virtually the very next day we booked some time in the studio and started writing some songs and choreographing our own routines. I was still at school at the time and the other girls all had full-time jobs (Keavy in the garage, Edele in a sports shop and Sinéad was working in a theatre), so we'd meet up at the Dance Centre to practise every single evening. A week or two later we were busy rehearsing when a TV crew, who were making a documentary about Digges Lane, spotted us and asked us to perform on the Saturday morning show they also produced – that weekend. Of course we were over the moon! The only problem was that we didn't have a song recorded, complete with music, as we'd been singing a capella until then!

So we pooled what money we had, and with the help of Keavy and Edele's mam and dad we went into the studio to do our very first recording. We actually recorded a few different songs. The one we performed on that first TV show was called 'A Shoulder To Cry On' and there was another one called 'True Love', which we literally wrote in about five minutes flat! Then it came to deciding on a name for our group. We came up with D'Zire, because at last we were getting to do exactly what we desired.

Keavy

As you can imagine, all four of us were really nervous that Saturday morning! We'd all performed on stage before, in various shows and dancing competitions, but never as a group, and appearing on Irish national television was a completely different matter altogether. We couldn't afford a stylist back then, so we got together our own outfits. Our clothes were quite tomboyish and we all wore matching boots, which set us back £120 *each*! I spent a whole week's wages on those boots. I actually still have them as a souvenir.

Anyway, the TV show went brilliantly. We were spotted on the programme and asked to support Boyzone on their next Irish tour — live on air! We were delighted!

We spent the next couple of weeks working like mad, perfecting our routines and preparing ourselves for our first ever concert performance. The gig was held at the Kings Hall in Belfast and I can remember the lights didn't go on for our first song and we were like HELLO?! Naturally we were extremely nervous, but we forgot all about our nerves once we were on stage and had a great time. The concert went really well for us.

The early days! This is when we were known as Sister. Check out Lindsay's blonde hair!

Sinead

There was a very special lady in the audience at that first concert, someone who would go on to shape the group's entire future. Her name was Kim Glover and she'd been put in touch with us by an associate of hers who had seen us on the Irish TV show. I can remember us all being so anxious about meeting Kim. We kept referring to her as 'The Lady from England.' We met up with her in a hotel in Dublin and then took her over to the Dance Centre to see us perform. We really wanted to impress her and didn't want to appear rude, so none of us spoke unless she spoke to us first! Kim eventually turned to us and said that people really wouldn't think it was rude at all if we went up to them and introduced ourselves, so these days we'll just go up and talk to anyone!

Soon afterwards she introduced us to her partner in management, Tommy J. Smith, and producer Ray Hedges, who we were later to work with. Ray is an amazingly talented man and we were all very excited. He took us into his recording studio and we started putting some new songs together. He and Kim suggested that we get a bit more experience of live audiences, so when we weren't spending time in the studio we'd go out and perform at schools, which was great fun.

It was very weird at first, particularly for the others, having to leave our families and friends behind in Ireland (I'd lived away from home before), but it was a sacrifice we knew we had to make if the band was to be a success. And with Kim and Ray on our side we knew that we were in exceptionally good hands.

B Edele

Kim decided that D'Zire wasn't the best of names and she suggested we called ourselves 'Sassy'. We discovered that there was already another band called Sassy, so we renamed ourselves again as Sister. At this point, we didn't have any kind of major recording deal. Kim thought it would be a good idea for us to go out and meet a few pop journalists, so on a hot summer's day we dropped into *Top Of The Pops* and *Live & Kicking* Magazines. We were so nervous. We came bounding into the magazine offices wearing these funny bouncy boot things and performed an unrehearsed version of 'Doh-a-Deer' from *The Sound Of Music* while bouncing around. The magazine staff must have thought we were absolutely crazy!

Meanwhile Ray and Kim were busy setting up meetings with various record companies, and arranged for us to meet Rob Stringer, who's the Managing Director of Epic Records, in a restaurant just outside London. As we still weren't entirely happy with our name, Ray had a brainwave. He said that he'd found us totally bewitching from the moment he first met us, and so — ta-da! — B*Witched was born. Rob Stringer thought he was coming to see us perform, but instead we'd arranged a kiddies' tea

party for him — complete with jelly, ice-cream, sweets and balloons! We wanted to do something different because record company bosses see loads of new bands every single week. I can remember us throwing marshmallows at him — how cheeky! Anyway, he was impressed by our liveliness and invited us to sing for him over at his offices in central London.

Before we knew it, he'd arranged for us to be signed to Epic on a development deal, giving us nine months to come up with some brand new songs. The first tracks we wrote were 'C'est La Vie' and 'To You I Belong'. We worked so hard over the next few weeks, often from early morning to very late at night. But it was all worth it as, with months left on our development deal, Rob called to say that Epic definitely wanted to release our album — and very soon! We were in a cafe when he phoned and we all burst out crying with happiness!

B★WITCHED

CHAPTER TWO
Edele

Family

My story begins on the day that Keavy and myself were born, in Dublin. Keavy was the first to pop out, and I soon followed, bringing the total of children in the Lynch family, at that point, to five. My dad Brendan is a car mechanic and has his own business, while my mam Noeleen is extremely creative and works from home doing all sorts of things like flower arranging and costume-making. Then there's our oldest sister Tara, our brother Shane, sister Allison, younger sister Naomi, Nana and nephew Dean. That's us, the Lynch clan, and as you can imagine there was never a quiet moment in our house while we were growing up! I was always very energetic as a kid. I was forever out playing in the garden or going swimming, dancing or doing gymnastics. I'd never sit still for long!

Keavy has always been and always will be my best friend.

Myself and Keavy in 1981. I think that's me on the left!

EDELE

People often say to us even now that it's difficult to tell us apart and I remember how our mam used to dress us in the same clothes when we were very little. Looking back on the pictures, it looks so cute! We once played a trick on our favourite schoolteacher, Miss Hickey. After three years she said she could tell us apart, so we swapped places in class just to confuse her and she didn't have a clue who was who! As we grew older, we gradually started wearing the same outfits, but in different colours.

Weren't we cute!

I'm often asked about the scar between my eyebrows (which is usually how people tell Keavy and myself apart). What happened was that on our third birthday, the two of us were being as lively as ever and pretending to be aeroplanes in our living room. We were spinning around quite fast and I slipped and knocked my head against the concrete step of our fireplace. Ouch! I was so young at the time that I can't really remember how much it hurt. Keavy and myself used to feel each other's pain when we were small. While I was in the operating theatre, my auntie Ann was minding Keavy and she cried from the second I went in there, to the moment I came out, saying she had a really bad headache.

Growing up in our house was absolutely brilliant. I honestly couldn't have asked for a better childhood — and that's mainly thanks to my mam and dad, who have always supported all their kids in whatever we wanted to do. Our entire family is extremely close, even though it's rare for us all to be together at the same time these days, but we spend a lot of time on the phone to each other. My mam and dad have always encouraged all of us to follow our dreams. Right now my sister Naomi is a European dancing champion, Allison lives in Boston, USA, where she works as a computer engineer, Tara is in a band called Fab! and of course Shane is in Boyzone.

Sisters!

School

Me in my first school uniform, 1982

My first memory of school was how, on the first day, the teachers wanted to separate Keavy and me, but mam and dad insisted that we remained together. Since that day we were always in the same class, which was great. I was a bit of chatterbox at school and was always getting told off for it, but I was generally a very good student. My favourite subjects were art and metalwork. In fact, I was the only girl in metalwork class and I was so embarrassed on the first day!

Outside school, I also started taking ballet classes, and then jazz classes with my oldest sister Tara. Together with Keavy, Tara and another girl, Pamela, we also had our own disco-dancing team, which was great fun. Our mam used to make all our costumes and we always looked cool; everyone used to say how brilliant our outfits were.

Every year, during the summer holidays, my mam and dad used to take us to Portugal, which was brilliant. We all used to love playing outside on the beach in the sunshine. One year though, when myself and Keavy were only a year old, our mam and dad decided to fly us all to America. I can remember they found our sister Allison crying in a corner. When they asked what was wrong she said she was crying because they'd said we were going to fly and she couldn't fly because she didn't have wings! It was so funny!

Music

All my life I've wanted to sing, and Keavy and I have always wanted to entertain together. I didn't necessarily want to be a pop star, but I knew deep down that I wanted to sing and entertain. I was always in our school plays and also got to perform some of my gymnastics on TV when I was younger. I used to love doing things like that. When we met Sinéad and Lindsay, the four of us immediately clicked both musically and socially and completely b*witched each other. We believe that faith brought us together.

My mam and dad are brilliant. They've always been behind me, no matter what. They have always had every faith in Keavy and me and they share our excitement at B*Witched's success. Obviously they do miss us because we're away from home so much these days, but they love coming to see us perform as often as they can — and sometimes bring the entire family with them! Our mam

tapes all of our TV appearances and keeps scrapbooks of all our interviews and photoshoots, which is a great memento of all we've achieved so far. Honestly, we're so busy we forget about half the interviews and stuff we do and it's always a real laugh reading through them when we get a few days off.

When I do get time off, I love staying at home, in my pyjamas, and sitting in front of the telly or meeting up with my friends. It's important to me that I keep in touch with all my friends, but sometimes it's hard to get to see everyone when I'm home because we get so little free time. My friends, like Peggie-Anne, Joanne and Mark, understand though, and we keep in touch all the time while B*Witched are on the road. I have to keep up on the gossip back home, you know!

Although I don't get much time to see my family or for myself these days, it really is all worth it. Each week that goes by I seem to fulfil yet another dream — being part of B*Witched is definitely a dream come true for me in itself.

B✲WITCHED

CHAPTER THREE

We'll give you such a thrill

 Sinead

Soon after signing our record deal with Epic, which is part of Sony Music, we were booked to appear on 911's UK tour. It was a pretty major tour for us, playing at some of the largest arena venues in the country. I can remember we had about two days to get our entire set together and we were all so worried that we'd forget the dance routines. We have a very creative choreographer, who incorporated traditional Irish and hip-hop into our routines to match the wide variety of musical styles in our songs.

The tour was brilliant! We had a great time, and it was good preparation for our showcase in London. The record company had hired The Talk Of London in Covent Garden and invited people from every TV and radio station, magazine and newspaper, as well as Sony representatives from all over the world, to come and see what B*Witched was all about. Our families flew over from Dublin to watch us too, and I can remember the whole place was packed. Sony had put a lot of time into decorating the venue in the B*Witched colours, orange and light blue, and there were B*Witched iced biscuits, sweets and loads of 'C'est

La Vie' flowers all around. The show itself was pretty spectacular too as Sony had arranged for these giant pyrotechnic glitter explosions to go off right at the end of our performance. It was amazing! Glitter has become one of our trademarks and we often carry glittery stars with us to sprinkle wherever we go.

 ## Edele

The next step for us was filming the video for what was to be our first single, 'C'est La Vie'. As we'd never made a video before, we found the whole experience really exciting — even though we were absolutely exhausted by the end of the day! We'd already had a meeting with the record company and decided that we'd all wear denim, and then set a stylist on the case finding outfits for us to wear for the video and the photoshoot for the single sleeve. I think the way we dress and the way we dance is probably the reason why we've been referred to as a 'tomboy band', a name we all quite like. It makes us different from all other pop groups and does actually suit our personalities.

You can't imagine how anxious we were when 'C'est La Vie' was released and how absolutely shocked and stunned we were when it entered the UK charts at number one! We honestly didn't expect it at all! At first we thought it was a joke, but when we discovered it was true, we all burst out crying and started hugging each other. We celebrated the following evening, when our record company took us out to dinner at Planet Hollywood in London, but sadly we couldn't party too much as we all had to be up extremely early the following morning.

Our diaries suddenly got very, very busy and our days became filled with photoshoots, interviews and TV appearances. I can remember us all watching ourselves on *Top Of The Pops* for the first time and thinking, 'is that really us?' As we needed to be in England so much, we'd all moved into a house together shortly after recording 'C'est La Vie', which is brilliant fun. We're all pretty good at looking after ourselves, so the place is fairly clean and tidy most of the time.

Lindsay

Making the video for 'Rollercoaster' is probably one of the hardest things we've ever done as we spent hours attached to these harnesses, pretending to be flying. All of the special effects were put in afterwards and we were completely blown away by the clip when we saw it for the first time. When 'Rollercoaster' topped the charts for us in September 1998, giving us our second number one in a row, we honestly couldn't believe it. I was in absolute shock! To celebrate, we were given the weekend off and we all went home to spend some time with our families.

It was around this time that Sony began to release our singles in Europe, which meant that a lot of our time was taken up on planes as we promoted the songs in countries such as France, Germany and Sweden. Of course we were really excited about visiting all of these places, but not nearly as excited as we were about the release of our debut album, *B*Witched*. As with everything concerning the group, making the album was very much a team effort. I remember us being in the studio with our producer Ray one day, when he speeded up our voices so that we sounded like chipmunks! Another time we thought he'd left for the day, when suddenly he burst through the door and drenched us with a fire extinguisher. It's no wonder he gets called 'The Madman'!

Well, our album was released in October and entered the UK album chart at number three, which was brilliant. To celebrate, we threw a Sunday lunchtime party at a restaurant in London called The Collection and invited loads of our friends from both within and outside the music industry. 911 were there and so was H from Steps and everyone seemed to have a brilliant time!

 Keavy

The next steps for us were trips to New York, Australia and Japan, where Sony was very interested in releasing our album. The trips went really well and we all managed to find plenty of time to go shopping. In New York, we did a showcase at an Irish pub called Connolly's, for Sony and the American media, which went down really well. When we returned to the UK, it was time to start thinking about our Christmas single, 'To You I Belong'. This song is really special to B*Witched because we wrote it about our mams and dads. New outfits were made specially for the video, a lot of which was filmed in a studio and then backdrops were added later. I can remember us all sitting in the boat in the middle of the room at about four in the morning pretending to be on that magical-looking lake!

Throughout 1998 B*Witched got to appear on so many different shows and we have immensely fond memories of them all. The first time we appeared on *Top Of The Pops*, it was everything we expected — except the studio is so much smaller than it looks on TV! We also loved appearing on the *Royal Variety Show* where we got to perform a B*Witched medley (in our snazzy new sequinned outfits!) and meet Prince Charles, who's a lovely man. Towards the end of the year, we also did a lot more travelling, firstly visiting Europe, followed by

Australia, New Zealand and then Japan and other Asian territories, all of which were fabulous experiences. We made a flying visit to Italy to appear at the MTV Europe Music Awards and promote 'Rollercoaster' in Rome, before flying back to the UK in time for the release of 'To You I Belong'.

Getting our third number one was just completely and utterly unbelievable — more than we could ever have hoped for. I remember how, for our appearance on the Christmas edition of *Top Of The Pops*, Edele and I swapped outfits and I tucked my fringe back and also wore red hair extensions like hers, so that we looked exactly the same. We fooled everyone — even Lindsay and Sinéad!

We had a couple of days off before Christmas, before flying out to the USA to perform with 'N Sync and tour the States, before returning to the UK to release 'Blame It On The Weatherman' and then jetting straight off to Europe to do some more promotion.

B*WITCHED

CHAPTER FOUR

Lindsay

Family

I was born in Athens, Greece. My mum, Sharon, is from Ireland and moved to Greece when she married my dad, Iannis, who owns a hotel in the Greek capital. I can truly say that I had an amazing childhood and look back on it with complete and utter happiness. I'm an only child, so I suppose I was spoilt to some degree, but not materially. Instead I was spoilt by receiving all my parents' attention and love.

I lived in Athens until I was 13, so I grew up speaking both English and Greek. A lot of other languages stem from Greek which came in handy at school when it came to studying Spanish, French and Latin. In fact I did Greek for my school Leaving Certificate and it brought my points right up! These days though, I don't get to use the language much, except when I'm talking to my dad or any of his family.

Ok, so now you can tell everyone you've seen me in the bath!

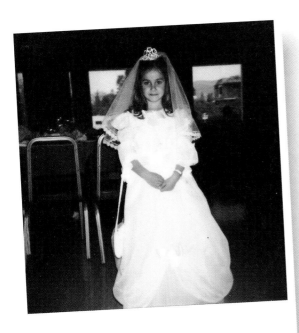

Me, age 7, in my Communion dress. I remember having frilly knickers on underneath!

Greece is such a cosmopolitan country to grow up in, as so many different nationalities live there — and of course it's absolutely steeped in ancient history. I love the lifestyle over there, being able to spend so much time outside in the brilliant sunshine.

In case you're wondering why my hair is blonde in my baby photos, well here's the story. I was actually born with a head of jet-black hair, which gradually got lighter and curlier until I was about three or four. Then, by the time I was 12 it had changed again and become long, dark and very straight. When I moved to Ireland, it went curly again. My natural hair colour these days is medium brown, but who knows, maybe it will change yet again, depending on where I live!

School

The first part of my education was spent in Greece. I was neither very loud nor very quiet in class: I was somewhere in between — I'd have a laugh with everyone else, but I was never the main ringleader or anything. My earliest memory is of my schoolfriends in

My mum made me this costume for the Christmas fair at kindergarten, where we all dressed up as fairies.

LINDSAY

Greece. Whenever it was anyone's birthday, the whole class would be invited to a party. Virtually every week there'd be another birthday party with balloons and clowns and cakes. I remember at one of mine, my mum gave everyone these giant lollies. They were huge and we all ran around licking them all afternoon.

My schooldays in Greece were very happy ones, but when I was 13 my mum decided to take me back to Ireland with her to complete my secondary education. I had actually been going to an English school in Greece, but she wanted me to gain an Irish Leaving Certificate. Sadly, my dad had to stay in Greece, as he couldn't leave his job running the hotel. I did really miss him, but we made sure we phoned home every single day. My mum and I would also go back to Greece at Easter, Christmas and for around three months every summer, which was lovely. I was always so excited to see him again. Of course, these days I see even less of both my parents because of my work, but I did manage to sneak a few days off last December when my mum was also out in Greece. To be honest though, I now consider both Greece and Ireland my home.

Anyway, back to school ...I wasn't very fond of maths — I found it so boring. Well one day in maths class I was really hungry, so I got this Mars bar out of my bag and each time the teacher turned to write on the board I'd have a quick nibble of it and then hide it under my desk. I caught my friend's eye across the room and whispered, asking if she would like some Mars bar. I cut it in half and flung her section across the room at her...except it went right past her head and hit the window with an almighty THUMP. It made such a loud noise! The teacher got really angry and said 'what was that?' and I said, 'A Mars bar, Sir. We were hungry!' He sent me outside for the rest of the lesson. Of course the whole class found it hysterically funny!

I completed my Junior Certificate and then the Leaving Certificate, getting 460 points out of a total of 600, which was more than enough to win me a place at Dublin's Trinity College. My parents were so pleased with me and I planned to go there to study for a degree in Business Studies. However, I decided to defer my place, because I'd just met up with Sinéad, Keavy and Edele and we were starting to get things going with the group. We'd rehearse every evening, which meant I would have had very little time to do my college work. Eventually I wrote to Trinity to say I wasn't coming back. Maybe one day I'll return to college — education is extremely important — but it would be to study something I'm curious about, like philosophy, rather than to get a degree to further my career.

Music

As a little girl, it was always my dream to become a pop star. When I was growing up I was always listening to my favourite records by Madonna, Kylie

Minogue, Michael Jackson and New Kids On The Block. I always had the radio on and I'd listen to absolutely any kind of music — even my dad's classical stuff. My first taste of showbiz came when I was about seven or eight, back in Greece, when I played the piano in the school Christmas concert. I loved every minute of being on the stage and took part in the show every year. My parents are both very musical. My dad plays the piano and accordion and my mum has a lovely singing voice and is a great dancer too. When I moved to Ireland, I joined the school choir and orchestra (playing the guitar and piano) and even conducted for a while! I also took part in some of my school's annual musicals as one of the brothers in *Joseph and the Amazing Technicolor Dreamcoat* and a dancer in *Little Shop of Horrors*.

My parents have always been extremely proud of me and really encouraged my obvious interest in music. They didn't ever specify any particular job that they wanted me to do; instead they let me make my own decision and I knew that they'd support me in whatever I chose. Even when I was applying to Trinity, I always intended to get together some demo tracks and send them off to record companies. I guess you could say music is in my blood, which is why I was so excited when the four of us met and decided to start a pop group of our own — my childhood dream was starting to become reality.

B★WITCHED

Around the world

Twelve months ago, we'd never have thought in our wildest dreams that we'd have visited so many brilliant countries and experienced so many different cultures. Here are a few of our favourite on the road memories...

IRELAND

Although Ireland's our home, we haven't been back there nearly as much as we'd have liked over the past year. We always receive a terrific response from our Irish fans and performing at Beat On The Street last summer was definitely a major highlight. The fans went absolutely mad when we came out on stage, which made us feel so proud!

AUSTRALIA

While in Australia, we met some of the cast of *Home & Away* and they were really nice. Best of all though was when I got to hold a koala bear. Aaw cute!

NEW YORK, USA

When we arrived at the airport in New York, we were all so impressed because this snazzy white limo had been sent to meet us. We felt like superstars! Until the car drove out onto the main road and we discovered that every other car was...yep, you guessed it, a white limo!

SWEDEN

Our first trip to Sweden seemed to be a bit jinxed. First of all we had to perform on a soaking wet stage because of the massive fountain display shown before us, and then we were given these salty-flavoured lollies, which were really disgusting!

PARIS, FRANCE

We had a wicked time at Disneyland Paris last autumn, as we got to go on absolutely every ride! Edele was a bit of a scaredy-cat, of course, but we all went on Space Mountain six times. It was really freezing over there so our record company bought us some white Mickey Mouse puffa jackets, which we still wear.

MILAN, ITALY

We went to last year's MTV Europe Music Awards and presented an award. However, before we read out the winner, I blew glitter over the envelope and it went straight in Lindsay's face. She was absolutely covered in glitter dust!

LOS ANGELES, USA

B*Witched got to support boy band 'N Sync, who are absolutely massive in America, and the whole tour was brilliant. We had the most incredible tour bus, which had 12 beds in it, and played in front of some of our biggest ever audiences. Funniest of all though were the shopping mall shows we did — imagine performing in the middle of a busy shopping centre!

LONDON, ENGLAND

I'm absolutely hopeless on the Underground and am always getting lost. Well one day, we all decided to go shopping and of course Lindsay and I lost Edele and Sinéad and didn't have a clue where we were going. We eventually made it back to our house about three hours later. The good thing was that by that time the others had already cooked dinner!

JAPAN

We all fell in love with Japan even though one of the TV shows we appeared on played a nasty trick on us. We were eating a traditional Japanese meal and they made us eat grasshoppers, which we didn't find funny at all!

ELBA, ITALY

Last summer we went to the island of Elba, which is absolutely gorgeous. Our hotel was right on the beach. It was fantastic. Anyway, none of us had expected it to be so hot, so we didn't bring any swimming costumes with us and we ended up running into the sea in our denims! The people on the beach thought we were absolutely crazy, but we didn't care at all!

SCOTLAND

We first played in Scotland on the 911 tour and during our set, a fan threw a teddy bear on stage for Spike. It was such a cute bear, that I just had to keep it!

B*WITCHED

CHAPTER FIVE

To you we belong

The amount of support we've had from our fans over the past year is absolutely incredible — and we really do appreciate it all immensely. We receive letters from all over the world now, mostly from people who want to let us know just how much they enjoy our music. And it's great to come home to sackloads of post, even though it takes us hours to get through it all now!

 ### Sinéad

I think B*Witched are really lucky because our fans are always so polite to us wherever we go. We've never really been mobbed as such — I don't think B*Witched are that kind of band. Instead people come up to us and ask for our autographs and have a quick chat, which is great.

In fact, our fans are so nice that we don't need a bodyguard at the moment, although we do always travel everywhere with our tour manager, Tommy, just to be on the safe side. Being recognized happened very gradually for all of us, which makes it a lot easier for us to deal with. I mean, imagine what it must be like to

Us with a popular Japanese TV presenter.

have people you've never seen before calling out your name in the street!

If I'm not with Lindsay, Keavy and Edele I hardly ever get recognized, which means I can still do really normal things like go on the Tube or pop to the shops without attracting too much attention. I'm quite shy by nature, so it's quite nice to be able to get on with everyday things without being mobbed everywhere I go.

Sinéad signs for a fan.

I have to tell you though, I once got sent half a pound of butter by a fan — don't ask me why! I haven't got a clue why anyone would want to send me that, but they did. That definitely goes down as the most bizarre gift I've ever received. We all love getting fan mail and we forward the addresses of any fan letters we receive to our information service, who then send out news of what we're up to.

Well, I hope that you'll continue listening to our music and if it brings a smile to your face, then that makes us very, very happy.

 ## Keavy

My first message to our fans is I hope you're enjoying this book. Thanks a million. We wouldn't be here without your support. You wouldn't believe how hectic things are for us at the moment. If fans write to me or Edele at our parents' house, our mam sometimes takes the time to send them autographs!

We obviously don't spend that much time at home in our house near London these days, but I remember one time when the four of us first moved in, there was a group of fans outside who kept knocking on the door all day long. We'd been having to answer the door all day, so when it came to dinner time, we pretended not to be in. The fans knew we were inside though and started getting a bit rough, saying they'd kick the door in if we didn't answer, so I opened the door and told

Chilling out while making the To You I Belong video.

them not to be so rude (very nicely of course). You should have seen their faces!

The weirdest thing for me is when people just stare at me because they recognize who I am. I'd far prefer it if they said 'hello' or something instead. When we were in Rome though, we met this group of fans who'd follow us absolutely everywhere. We'd leave a place before them, but by the time we got to our next destination, they'd already be there waiting for us — even in the pouring rain!

As Sinéad already said, we can still lead relatively normal lives and do normal everyday things without needing security men with us all the time. Although when I was at home last Christmas, I went into town with my friends Mark and Terry to visit my best friend, Sandra, at work. When we left, everyone was asking her if they were my bodyguards, which we all thought was really funny!

Lindsay

It may sound corny when bands say that they love their fans, but honestly, it's true! If you guys didn't like B*Witched's music, we definitely wouldn't be where we are today. And we do genuinely enjoy meeting up with fans at roadshows, gigs and TV appearances — it's always good to get feedback. It's especially nice, when we're away from home and missing our families, to come out on stage and face a massive crowd all cheering for us and singing along to our songs. It's easily one of the best feelings the world!

People often ask us what it's like to be famous, and to be honest I still feel like exactly the same person. I don't ever wake up and think, 'gosh, I'm famous!' B*Witched's popularity grew quite gradually. We were performing at schools long before the release of 'C'est La Vie' and everything's just grown from there. Signing my first ever autograph was a bit weird though, simply because someone had actually recognized me and thought I was important enough!

There's absolutely no hiding from fans, however. I remember one day I was out shopping in Dublin, just after 'C'est La Vie' had been released. I was in Knickerbox, completely preoccupied with underwear, when the song came on in the shop. To this day I'm not sure if the sales assistants played it deliberately, or if it was purely coincidental, but I went puce and had to leave the shop immediately!

 ## Edele

It's weird when people notice us in countries we've never even visited before! I remember it was really strange when we first went to Australia, because everyone seemed to know exactly who we were, just through having seen the

'Rollercoaster' and 'C'est La Vie' videos before we arrived. It was mad!

When we travel to a country for the first time, none of us expect to be recognized at all, which is why our trip to Singapore was so amazing. The fans over there followed us absolutely everywhere! At one point they even managed to discover our hotel rooms, by knocking on every door on every floor until they found us! We couldn't believe it!

They also hired taxis so that they could trail our every move, and the same group of fans would be at every TV studio or photoshoot we went too. In fact, they seemed to know exactly what we were up to before we did!

We often get asked if our boy fans are any different from our girl fans and the truthful answer is not really, although some of the boys do act a bit differently, they're more reserved. Would I date a fan? Well, not if he was only interested in me because I'm in B*Witched, and I guess there's always a fear of that being the case even with friendship. If he genuinely liked me as a person, well then who knows?

One thing I would like to say to the fans is thanks a million for all your support. We couldn't have done any of this without you! You give us so many dreams and I hope we do the same for you.

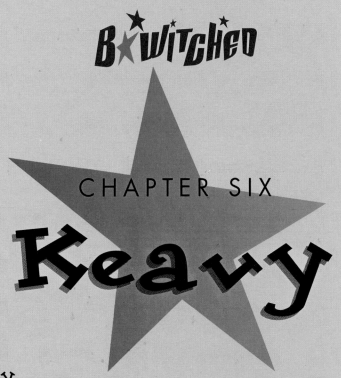

B*WITCHED

CHAPTER SIX
Keavy

Family

Being sisters, mine and Edele's stories are very similar. We were born in the Coombe Hospital in Dublin and were inseparable from day one. Our mam and dad would dress us both the same, which some people think is mean, but we both loved it. In fact — and I only found this out when I was choosing photos for this book — our mam entered us in a bonnie baby contest and we won first prize. I guess that counts as our first ever award! Edele and myself have always been very close to our parents and I still feel that I can talk to them about absolutely anything. I had a lot of fun growing up with them and I love getting time to spend with them now. They've always been my idols and I've always said that I won't get married until I find someone to love in the same way my mam and dad love each other.

Betcha never thought you'd see myself and Edele in dressses!

As a child I was always very happy, extremely playful, energetic and sporty. I'd say I was probably a bit shyer than Edele, and still am, but we both really had a great childhood. My first ever memory was when I was three years old and in hospital with pneumonia. I remember I wasn't allowed to get out of bed and all the other children on my ward were. I also remember the day my parents brought my little sister Naomi home from hospital, just after she'd been born. I thought she was absolutely amazing, so perfect and I was her big sister! I guess I've always loved babies and, coming from quite a large family myself, I'd like to have four or five kids of my own someday.

Me and Edele at a disco dancing competition in April 1994

Our family has always been extremely close, which is why I miss everyone like mad these days. Being away from home so much is definitely a down side of being in a band, but I suppose it's a sacrifice that has to be made as we're now fulfilling our dreams. At least I have one of my family, Edele, with me all the time. There's definitely a very special bond between us. Sometimes we come out with the same things at the same time. It's weird!

School

My first school photo

I was always very shy at school. On my first day I remember being brought into the class by my sisters Tara and Allison and I absolutely bawled my eyes out when they went to leave. Both Edele and myself worked very hard, and were always in the highest class until we reached the fourth year. It was a transition year and we didn't do much, so we became bored and started being a bit louder and chatting in class.

My favourite subject was always P.E. I loved doing sport. I played on the school volleyball team for a while and won medals for gymnastics and swimming. I'm also pretty good at kick-boxing, which I started learning when I was 17. I'm now a blue belt. I would have trained for my purple belt, but I just didn't have time when we moved to England when B*Witched took off. My instructor, Martin Farrell, always wanted me to take part in competitions, but I don't agree with people getting in the ring and hurting each other. I do know how to look after myself, but hope I'm never in a situation where I have to use my kick-boxing skills. Martin is still a great friend of mine and he's really proud of B*Witched.

I loved the school holidays. One year in Ireland we went out on my dad's boat on the River Liffey, which runs through the centre of Dublin. My friend Mark and I got hungry, so we stopped the boat, climbed up the steps and nipped into McDonalds in our wetsuits. It was so funny — the staff had to mop up after us as we were dripping river water everywhere!

Music

I guess you could say we're a very musical family. My sister Tara is in a group called Fab! and my big brother Shane is in Boyzone. My grandad used to play the fiddle, and my uncle Ciaran and his family are world-class drummers. Our mam's also musical and plays the guitar. As for myself, well, I first started dancing when I was about 13. I used to dance with Tara, who suggested that I go down to the dance centre in Digges Lane, Dublin and take jazz dancing lessons. I was actually late for my first ever class because I didn't want to attend without the proper shoes and trousers. My mam, dad and myself had to run around town and get some, but when I turned up, no-one else in the class had the right uniform anyway!

I didn't ever want to study for dancing exams or anything — I just wanted to dance. As well as jazz, I began tap classes and then Edele and I both started to learn hip-hop. We loved it and after a short while formed a hip-hop dance group called BOOM with our friends Peggie-Anne, Mark, Graham and Danny and we performed at promotional events for things like Sony PlayStation and Coca-Cola. Eventually we started teaching dance classes, which was hard work, but we thoroughly enjoyed it. Myself, Tara, Edele and Naomi also formed a disco-dancing group called Starlight and entered loads of competitions.

Before B*Witched, the only band I'd ever been in was a marching band called the Dublin Allstars. I played the saxophone and twirled a flag, which was great fun! I'd also had a couple of jobs, firstly working in a sports shop

KEAVY

and then as a trainee mechanic in my dad's garage. I actually worked there for just over a year, until that now famous day when I met Sinéad and we decided to follow our dreams and form a group. Looking back, I can't believe how much we've achieved in so little time. But dreams are still coming true for us. I never dreamed I'd be on a tour bus in America writing a book, but here I am!

B*WITCHED

CHAPTER SEVEN
Rollercoaster of love!

Here's where we get to talk about one of our favourite subjects...love!

 Keavy

Have you ever been in love?

I once thought I was. When I do find true love, I'll definitely never let it go.

Who was your first boyfriend?

His name was Karl and I went out with him for 2½ years. He lives down my way and we still keep in touch now.

Tell us about your first kiss...

I was about 12, but I don't remember if I enjoyed it or not. The first time someone gave me a French kiss, I thought I was going to be sick!

What's the most romantic thing a boy's ever done for you?

Someone once bought me flowers and a really cute teddy bear.

Is it hard to have a boyfriend and be in B*Witched?

Definitely, because we'd be away from each other so much. But I do believe that there is someone out there for everyone and I'm sure one day it'll just hit me and I'll fall madly in love.

What do you look for in a boy?

Someone who makes me laugh and smile. Someone who would look after me, but also let me look after them and who's not ashamed to cry.

 ## Sinéad

How would you define 'Love'?

Love is a very exciting thing and involves a lot of respect, trust and loyalty.

Have you ever been in love?

I've thought I've been in love a few times, but looking back I realize that I wasn't really.

Who was your first boyfriend?

I won't tell you his name, but I went out with him for ten months when I was 16.

What about your first kiss?

I think I was about 15. I was absolutely terrified!

When did you last have a romantic night out?

I had a hot date last Christmas, but I'm not going out with anyone at the moment, although I do have my eye on someone.

What's the most romantic thing a boy's ever done for you?

I once stayed up talking all night long with this young man, we got on brilliantly. Then, the next day we played pool and he let me win!

What do you look for in a boy?

Someone spontaneous who I can have a laugh with. And someone who can give me lots of affection.

 ## Edele

How would you define love?

Love is 100% trust. It's when you always want to put someone else first and it's something money can't buy.

How romantic are you?

I love romance! I think being spontaneous and giving surprises is very romantic.

Who was your first boyfriend?

He was a guy I went to school with called Patrick.

Can you remember your worst kiss?

One time I went to kiss this guy and had my eyes closed, so I didn't realize that he'd turned his head! that wasn't very nice.

What's the best way to flirt?

By making a bit more eye contact than usual. That usually works!

When did you last have a romantic night out?

It was probably around Valentine's Day 1998. I was taken out to dinner and given a beautiful bunch of red roses.

What do you look for in a boy?

A sense of humour and a bit of romance. I like a boy who's punctual, but most of all the chemistry between us both has to be right.

 ## Lindsay

Are you a romantic person?

Yes, definitely. I like little things like sending cards for no reason, or going out for dinner and being given flowers.

Who was your first boyfriend?

When I was 16 I met this boy in Greece during the summer holidays, but then I had to come back to Ireland. It wasn't just a holiday romance though, because I also consider Greece to be my home.

What about your first kiss?

It was with a boy at the back of the school bus when I was 11. I remember getting off the bus when it reached my street and seeing him still looking at me through the window.

Do you have a boyfriend?

No. Sometimes I wish I did, but I don't need a boyfriend to feel complete. My career is my priority at the moment.

Have you been on any disastrous dates?

Yes. I met this guy when I was out in Ireland and gave him my phone number. He called the next day and we arranged to meet, but I just didn't fancy him enough. I felt so awkward all night.

What do you look for in a boy?

Someone who's caring, thoughtful, has plenty of ambition and is, above all, affectionate.

B*WITCHED

CHAPTER EIGHT
Sinéad

Family

It's my turn now to tell you all about my life so far. Well, I was born in Dublin and my family moved to Newbridge when I was a few months old. My dad Eamonn is an electrician by trade and has his own company, while my mum Barbara owns a lingerie shop in Newbridge, Co. Kildare. I'm the eldest child and have two sisters, Elaine and Ailish and one brother, Paul, and I'd say we all get on really well. As a child, I was always very focused and knew exactly what I wanted to do. Like I'd tell my mum I'd clean my bedroom when I wanted to and not when she wanted me too. I guess I could be a bit cheeky at times!

My parents would probably say that I'm very independent and extremely ambitious and serious about everything I do. At times though, I do go off into my own little dreamworld and can also be quite forgetful. The other girls are always having to remind me to remember all my personal belongings whenever we're on the road — but I am getting a lot better! As a child, I always had a very vivid imagination. My first memory is of the time my family visited a place in Ireland called the Ring of Kerry. It was really foggy and there was a cross at the

top of the hill. I was absolutely convinced that we were in heaven.

Another fond memory of mine is of my First Holy Communion, which took place when I was seven. I can remember getting up to find that my mum had laid my entire outfit out on my bed — right down to the frilly knickers! I had a parasol, the works! Getting dressed that day was like a ceremony in itself. I had a lovely short dress and my best friend, Suzanne Hennessy, had a long dress and we seemed to spend most of the day having our photos taken. I felt as though I was a princess!

School

I was pretty good at school and did actually enjoy it. I was always the smallest in the class, so to make up for it I'd be outspoken. Suzanne and I remained best friends all through our school days and still keep in touch now. My favourite subjects were always French and music, although I did work hard in all my subjects and ended up with pretty good grades.

Although music was one of my favourites, we did once play a trick on our teacher. Two of my friends hid in a closet in the classroom and I was sitting quite near it. Anyway, for some reason the teacher needed to move the cupboard and when he did, my friends jumped out and gave him the fright of his life! It was really funny, but of course we got into trouble for messing around.

I quite enjoyed playing sports at school, but I felt I was too small to get involved with many of the activities. Looking back, I realize how silly that was. I did win a medal for hurdling – I think I've still got that medal somewhere at home. In my Transition year I also won Schoolgirl of the Year.

I started dancing when I was 4, and from 8 to 13 I took Irish dancing lessons outside school with a lovely lady called Mary Donaghue. She'd enter my dance class in competitions and we had the most amazing traditional green costumes. Myself and my sister Elaine had danced together for years (she has a beautiful voice and is now studying German and Travel in Dublin). I then began to learn jazz and tap and when I turned 15 I started taking jazz and ballet classes in the centre of Dublin. I felt so grown up being allowed to travel on my own from our home in Newbridge to the city centre!

It became more than obvious to me that dancing was going to be part of my future. I was absolutely passionate about it, and jumped at the chance when I won a year's scholarship to the prestigious London Studio Centre in King's Cross. I learnt virtually every

My Irish dancing class. I'm second from the right in the front row.

kind of dancing there — ballet, tap, jazz, character — in fact, the only kind of dancing I wasn't taught was breakdancing. I didn't have a feel for hip-hop, but dancing with the girls soon got me into the vibe of it.

Music

Like the other members of B*Witched, I always knew I'd follow a career connected with entertaining. I took music and drama classes at Newbridge College every summer until I was 15 and my first major role was playing the Wizard in *The Wizard Of Oz*. I had a whale of a time! I also took speech and drama classes with a very inspiring lady, Edele Mulligan, who always had great faith in me.

I've always loved music and started playing the piano when I was eight years old. I can remember dancing around my bedroom singing along to Wham! records (in fact, I still love George Michael), and I was also really into the Kids From Fame!

When I finished school, I found myself some work at the Olympia and Gate theatres in Dublin and also got myself a few parts as an extra on TV. My parents were always very supportive. They knew that I only wanted to perform and encouraged me to follow my dream. Along the way though I did have to take up other jobs as a shop assistant and doing telesales, but I knew these would only be temporary and that I had enough determination and drive to make it as a performer.

I absolutely love being part of B*Witched, even though I don't get much time to spend at home with my family and close friends, which can be hard to deal with at times. I think all of us get homesick now and again. I do still keep in touch with my friends from Ireland and I spent a brilliant

SINEAD

day pampering myself just before Christmas. One of my friends, R.K., came over to London and we went on a mad shopping spree, which is something I hardly ever have time to do at the moment. By the end of the day, I was completely worn out and needed a really long, hot, relaxing bath with lavender oil. Mmm.

As you can probably guess, I'm completely over the moon at the success B*Witched have experienced so far. It really is an amazing feeling to be living the life and fulfilling the ambitions you've always dreamed of. It's made me realise how important it is to have dreams of your own and shown me that if you persevere, they can really become reality. But I never forget exactly how lucky B*Witched have been.

B★Witched

CHAPTER NINE

We four girls are here to stay!

All four of us are really amazed at the way B*Witched has taken off over the past twelve months, and we've got loads of plans for the future. We've already started writing and recording our second album, which should hopefully be available at the end of 1999. There isn't too much we can say about it at the moment, except that it'll contain a real mixture of tracks, which we hope you'll like. Our producer Ray Hedges has been here with us in the USA while we've been writing this book, and we plan to do some more recording with him during his trip. We recorded some of the last album in a hotel room in London, so who knows what strange locations our new album will be made in!

Our biggest dream in 1999 is to stage a major B*Witched tour. That would be totally amazing as we love being on stage. At the moment it looks as though this could happen around November or December this year, so we're keeping our fingers firmly crossed. We can't wait to start getting a full live show together and we've already got loads of ideas, so it's going to be really cool.

Obviously none of us can predict what the future holds for B*Witched. Look

WE FOUR GIRLS ARE HERE TO STAY

at 1998! None of us expected to achieve such a massive degree of success, even in our wildest dreams! We still can't believe that our first three singles went straight in at number one! What we do know though, is that while you're still enjoying our music, we'll continue performing and making you happy. We're living out our dreams. And B*Witched are definitely here to stay!

B★WITCHED

25 B★witching facts!

★ Sinéad has won medals for gymnastics, hurdles and running!

★ To date, B★Witched have sold a staggering 2 million singles and 1.5 million albums worldwide!

★ Edele's favourite song in the world in 'The Bangles' 'Eternal Flame'!

★ Lindsay does a wicked impersonation of a fire alarm.

★ If you're making Sinéad a pizza, forget the olives as she can't stand them!

★ Keavy is afraid of rats!

★ B★Witched would all love to star in a Disney film.

★ Edele's scared of creepy-crawlies — especially spiders!

★ When they were very little, Keavy and Edele blew up their mum's car by mistake. Fortunately, neither of them were hurt.

★ Lindsay has three dogs, Leah, Snoopy and Huskey and two cats, Cheeky and Chubby!

★ Edele's full name is Edele Claire Christina Edwina Lynch

★ One of B★Witched's fans, Christina, adopted a bush-baby for the girls as a Christmas present!

★ Sinéad's full name is Sinéad Maria O'Carroll

★ Keavy and Edele's pets include two ducks, Jack and Jill and some tropical fish!

★ The girls say they don't have much time to spend with boys anymore. Aaw.

★ Sinéad would spend her last fiver on a call card so that she could have a chat with her folks!

★ Keavy's full name is Keavy-Jane Elizabeth Annie Lynch

★ Lindsay cooks a mean spaghetti Bolognese — even though she can't scoff it herself as she doesn't eat red meat!

★ The girls wrote 'To You I Belong' for their mams and dads.

★ Keavy's the biggest joker in B★Witched and always has the others in stitches!

★ Sinéad's belly-button's an inny!

★ Lindsay's full name is Lindsay Gael Christian Elaine Armaou

★ Keavy uses a purple and white toothbrush

★ Collector's item alert! In Japan, B★Witched have been turned into cartoon characters on promotional stickers!

B★WITCHED

UK DISCOGRAPHY

SINGLES

Title	Release Date	Chart Position
C'est La Vie	May 25 1998	1
Rollercoaster	September 21 1998	1
To You I Belong	December 7 1998	1
Blame It On The Weatherman	March 8 1999	?

ALBUM

B*Witched	October 12 1998	3

AUTHOR'S ACKNOWLEDGEMENTS

Many thanks to: Kim Glover, Tommy Jaysmith, Joanna Burns, Ailsa Robertson, Tasha Browning and especially Edele, Keavy, Lindsay & Sinéad.

PHOTOGRAPHY CREDITS

© Julian Barton 2, 4, 11, 12, 13, 14, 16b, 19, 21, 24, 25, 26, 29, 31, 32r, 36b, 38, 42, 45b, 46, 47, 51, 52, 54b, 56, 57, 59, 60-61

© Tim Bret Day 9

© Elaine Constantine 60, 40-41, 49

© Kim Glover 10, 17t, 22, 23, 32l, 33, 35, 36t, 37, 39

© Tommy Jay 10

Photographs on pages 15, 16t, 17b, 27, 28, 43, 44, 45t, 53, 54t, 55 courtesy of B*Witched and their parents.